EXPLORING OAHU

WITH

KIDS

A Jr. Travelers Series Memory Book

Publication and Copyright 2013
Travelers Series Publishing, LLC
11858 Bernardo Plaza Ct.
Suite 230
San Diego, CA 92128
Printed in the United States

JR. TRAVELERS SERIES

Dear Jr. Traveler,

We hope you're excited about a great vacation! Your memory book is filled with many challenges, including pictures, trivia, scavenger hunts and collections. It can be fun to work with your family or friends to complete the challenges together. Do your best, but remember that the most important part of any activity is to collect the sights, smells, and sounds of your family adventure.

Be sure to visit us online at TravelersSeries.com to learn about other Jr. Travelers Series products and destinations. Wherever your family adventure takes you, we're glad you're taking us along for the ride. Happy traveling!

Sincerely,

The Bowers and Medley families

Co-Founders, Travelers Series Publishing

 DO IT!

Sometimes you will want to collect things that won't fit on the pages of your memory book. Other times, you will visit places that are not in the book. Before you leave on your trip you need to create a "Souvenir Saver" to store mementos like pictures, tickets, receipts, menus and more. You can also attach them to the blank pages at the back of this book.

1. Find a manilla envelope with a string or metal clasp.

2. Decorate the envelope with drawings or other artwork.

3. Write "Souvenir Saver" on the envelope.

4. Use your Souvenir Saver to collect mementos from your trip!

OAHU

PASSPORT TO
OAHU, HAWAII
USA

Tape your favorite
Hawaii picture here.

Tip: Be sure to take your pictures sideways,
because your Jr. Travelers Memory book is
designed to fit pictures horizontally.

CHALLENGES

Surfboard Count CHALLENGE!

Hawaii is famous for its large waves and scores of surfers. With so many great beaches to catch a wave, Hawaiians love to shoot the curl. You will see locals and tourists alike sharing their love of surfing. Count how many surfboards you see during your trip - in the water, on the beach and on top of cars. Use the box to the right to tally up your sightings and write the total on the line below the box!

Total: _____

Tiki Statue CHALLENGE!

The word "tiki" refers to stone and wood carvings made in a human shape. These statues are a part of Polynesian Mythology and can be found throughout the Hawaiian islands. Today, you can find just about anything made with a tiki - placemats, cups, pens, key chains, t-shirts, candy and more! Count how many different tikis you find and write down the most interesting tiki, take a picture and store it in the Souvenir Saver!

Total: _____

The most interesting tiki I saw was: _____

Aloha State Flower CHALLENGE!

Hawaii is full of exotic flowers and they come in a seemingly never-ending array of bright and beautiful colors! Enjoying the floral diversity of Hawaii is another way to truly appreciate the magic of the islands. As you explore this tropical state try to find two different types of flowers for each of the colors listed to the right. Check the box when you find each of the two flowers and do your best to label the type of flower you found by asking those around you or looking up the flower on the internet. Take pictures of your favorite flowers and store them in the Souvenir Saver or tape them to the Aloha Memories pages at the end of this book.

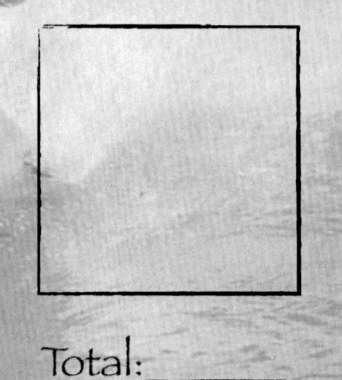

	Flower #1	Flower #2
Red	☐ _____	☐ _____
Yellow	☐ _____	☐ _____
Green	☐ _____	☐ _____
Pink	☐ _____	☐ _____
White	☐ _____	☐ _____
Purple	☐ _____	☐ _____
Multi	☐ _____	☐ _____
Orange	☐ _____	☐ _____

CHALLENGES

Rainbow Chasers
CHALLENGE!

Hawaii is a tropical paradise. It rains a lot to stay so green! All of the moisture in the air creates lots of rainbows! Tally all the rainbows you see during your visit using the box to the right. At the end, write down your total. Whenever possible, take a picture of the rainbows you see and store your favorites on the pages in the back of this book or in the Souvenir Saver.

Total: _____

Warning Sign
CHALLENGE!

WARNING

Throughout the islands, there are all sorts of signs that tell you what is coming, what might be coming and what you should be looking for. Many of these signs are unique to Hawaii. As you learn about Hawaii and the places you travel, keep an eye out for the most interesting signs you can find. Take a picture of your favorites and use the space to the left to design your very own sign.

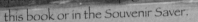

Explore the Terrain CHALLENGE!

Hawaii is famous for more than its world famous beaches! One of the cool things about the Hawaiian Islands is their proximity to many different terrains. In under an hour, you can travel from the beach, to dry/arid volcanoes, to tropical rainforests, mountains and sprawling valleys. During your trip, try to visit each of the following: (1) the beach, (2) the mountains, (3) a volcano, and (4) the rainforest. Write down where you visited on the lines to the right. Then take a picture and keep it in your Souvenir Saver.

1. _____ 2. _____

3. _____ 4. _____

aloha! Hawaii

☆ GET IT!

Hawaii is a beautiful state that is waiting for you to take memorable pictures. Keep your camera nearby – you never know what you will see! Try to take pictures of all of the items listed on these two pages. Choose a favorite toy or stuffed animal for the Bonus below.

BONUS!

Try to get a favorite toy or stuffed animal in every picture you take during your trip.

Checklist

- ☐ You taking a picture
- ☐ You and a tiny dog
- ☐ Someone sleeping
- ☐ You in a tree
- ☐ Your Hawaiian name
- ☐ Your worst vacation day

- ☐ You, upside down
- ☐ Your craziest outfit
- ☐ You jumping on the bed
- ☐ You and a new friend
- ☐ You wearing a snorkel
- ☐ Eating food on a stick

- ☐ You on someone's shoulders
- ☐ Your hands or feet in water
- ☐ A grumpy grown-up
- ☐ You in the car or airplane
- ☐ You by your front door
- ☐ You sitting inside your suitcase

Tape your favorite picture here.

Tip: You can use a mirror to take a picture of yourself taking pictures!

aloha! hawaii

- [ ] An ice cream shop
- [ ] A helicopter
- [ ] A Hawaii state flag
- [ ] You floating in water
- [ ] A statue
- [ ] A giant wave
- [ ] A red door
- [ ] A grave marker
- [ ] Snorkel Bob's
- [ ] A tourist t-shirt
- [ ] Any city hall
- [ ] An ABC Store
- [ ] People kissing
- [ ] You hula dancing
- [ ] A police car
- [ ] A tropical garden
- [ ] A purple sign
- [ ] A place of worship
- [ ] A flower necklace

Tape your favorite picture here.

Tip: Make sure you keep all of your other pictures in the Souvenir Saver!

- [ ] You in a grass skirt
- [ ] A person riding a bike
- [ ] Something with stripes
- [ ] You on a Boogie Board
- [ ] Seaweed
- [ ] A cupcake store

- [ ] Bubbles
- [ ] A train
- [ ] A horse
- [ ] A blimp
- [ ] A dragon
- [ ] A fountain

- [ ] A turtle
- [ ] An angel
- [ ] A squirrel
- [ ] A pineapple
- [ ] A billboard
- [ ] A fancy car

ARRIVING IN HAWAII

Tape a picture of how you got to Hawaii.

Tip: People arrive in Hawaii everyday by airplane and sometimes by boat.

Tape your hotel key.

Tip: If you didn't stay in a hotel, tape any memento of where you stayed during your time in Hawaii.

✋ DO IT!
Draw a picture of a special Hawaiian landmark.

Place cool stamp here!

THIS SIDE FOR MESSAGE

Date _____

Dear _____,

POST CARD

PLACE STAMP HERE

Hawaii is totally amazing and the weather is great!

The weather was: _____

I went with: _____

I felt.

ARRIVING IN HAWAII

 **DO IT!**
Draw your idea for a
Hawaiian flag.

Tape a picture of a
Hawaiian freeway sign.

EAST

378

WRITE IT!
Write and illustrate a poem or
short story about a child
your age who lives in Hawaii.
Store your work in the
Souvenir Saver.

☆ **GET IT!**
☐ Hawaii map
☐ Parking receipt

FIND IT!
Try to spot these on the road:
☐ Turtle crossing sign
☐ Airport sign

DO IT!
Write four things you've never seen before.

_____
_____
_____
_____

THE BEACH

Tape a picture
of the beach.

Tip: See how many of the items below
you can capture in one picture.

Beach Name:

🔭 FIND IT! at the Beach

Find these items at the beach:

- ☐ Bird
- ☐ Rock
- ☐ Shell
- ☐ Litter
- ☐ Feather
- ☐ Fish
- ☐ Beach ball
- ☐ Seaweed
- ☐ Lifeguard
- ☐ Surfboard
- ☐ Sand crab
- ☐ Catamaran

Tape a picture
of the beach.

Tip: Lighting for pictures at the beach is
best during sunrise and sunset.

Design a Surfboard

Some of the world's most famous
surfboard designs can be seen in
Hawaii. Create your own design
by coloring and decorating the white
surfboard here.

✋ DO IT! Build a Sand Castle

Build a castle with sand
and containers.
Decorate it with shells.
Take a picture and store
it in the Souvenir Saver.

Dig a moat and a
channel from your
castle to the ocean.
When the tide comes
in, it will fill your moat.

Do It! Aloha! What did you say?

Open air markets are rich with Hawaiian culture and history. Many words have several meanings, like Aloha, which can mean hello, goodbye, love, kindness and more! Try to use these Hawaiian phrases while shopping in the market:

- ☐ Yes = Ae (eye)
- ☐ Please = Olu olu (OH-loo OH-loo)
- ☐ Hello = Aloha (ah-LO-ha)
- ☐ No = Aole (AH-oh-lay)
- ☐ Excuse me = E ia nei (Ey EE-ah NAY-ee)
- ☐ Thank you = Mahalo (ma-HA-lo)
- ☐ Goodbye = Aloha (ah-LO-ha)
- ☐ How are you? = Pehea oe? (pey-HEY-ah OH-ey)

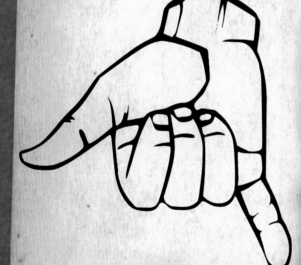

Hang Loose!

Hawaiians use the Shaka Sign – which means hang loose – to show their "Aloha Spirit." Color the Shaka sign below.

Tip: Take a picture of you buying a souvenir.

Aloha!

INTERNATIONAL MARKET PLACE

FARMERS' MARKET

👓 FIND IT!
Flower Market

Walk through the farmers' market
and find these flowers or plants:

- ☐ Rose
- ☐ Iris
- ☐ Hibiscus
- ☐ Bonsai
- ☐ Orchid
- ☐ Lavender

- ☐ Gardenia
- ☐ Lavender
- ☐ Anthurium
- ☐ Carnation
- ☐ Firecracker Plant
- ☐ Bird of Paradise

Tape a picture of
a farmers' market.

Tip: Take a picture in front of the strangest food you see.

The Farmers' Market sells everything from produce to toys to ice cream.
Make a list of all the things you want to buy. Then draw them in the crate.

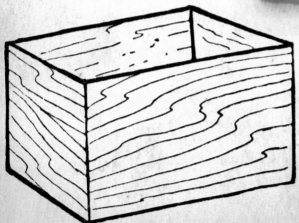

_____

_____

_____

PLANTATION

Tape a picture from the plantation.

Tip: Get a picture showing you as a farmer on the plantation.

? ANSWER IT! ?

What are four uses for the fruit grown below?

_____

_____

_____

✋ DO IT!

Design a meal using plantation crops. Be sure you label your creation!

🔍 FIND IT!
Plantation Photo Hunt

Find and take a picture of these things! You'll find some only in the feeding area.

- ☐ Pineapple
- ☐ Fruit Juice
- ☐ Tractor
- ☐ Plantation Animal
- ☐ Farmer

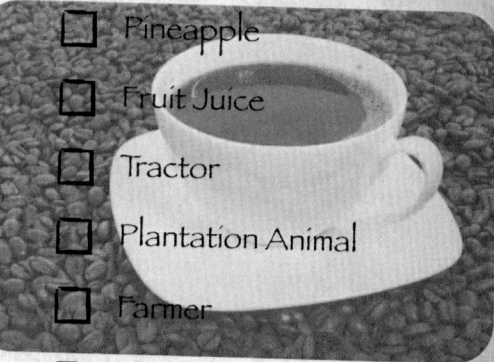

- ☐ Flower
- ☐ Plantation Sign
- ☐ Two Different Varieties of Plantation Food
- ☐ Gift Shop
- ☐ Map of the Plantation
- ☐ Bathroom Item made from Plantation Product

Hawaiian Snow

✋ DO IT!
Design Your Own Hawaiian Snow

Draw your very own Hawaiian Snow concoction in the cup below. To the side, write all of the flavors that you included in your creation. Be sure to give it a name!

Tape a picture of you eating a Hawaiian Snow.

Tip: Take one picture when you start and one when you finish – what a mess!

Name _____

Flavors _____

✋ DO IT! Flavor Mix-up!

Hawaiian Snow comes in many different flavors. Unscramble the following Hawaiian Snow Flavors.

mtWnlaereo _____

maniCnon _____

reyCrh _____

trbySwerar _____

oRto ereB _____

totonC danCy _____

naiP dolaCa _____

bBblue mGu _____

RAINFOREST

Tape a picture of the rainforest.

Tip: Take a picture of a very interesting plant, or you by the water.

DO IT! Skipping Stone Challenge

There are often small creeks or rivers in the rainforest. Skipping stones in the water can be a lot of fun. Find the smoothest, flattest and roundest rocks you can and see how many times you can skip stones on top of the water. Write down the number of "skips" on the lines below.

1st Try _____

2nd Try _____

3rd Try _____

4th Try _____

Most Ever _____

🔭 FIND IT! in the Rainforest

Find these items in the rainforest:

⚠ WARNING

Flash Flood!
Be alert, water may rise without warning.
Fast moving water may result in serious injury or death.

☐ Bird
☐ Litter
☐ Insect
☐ Sign
☐ Log

☐ Fish
☐ Feather
☐ Wild animal
☐ Colored rock
☐ Large boulder

☐ Frog
☐ Slug
☐ Leaf
☐ Lizard
☐ Plant growing

ALOHA SHIRT

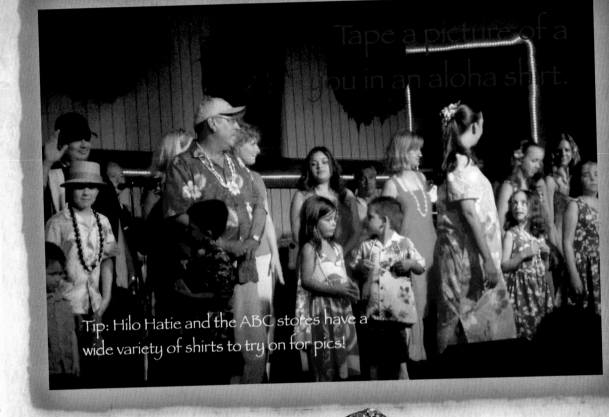

Tip: Hilo Hatie and the ABC stores have a wide variety of shirts to try on for pics!

Tape a picture of you in an aloha shirt.

Aloha Shirt

Aloha shirts are also called Hawaiian shirts. This style was started in Hawaii and this first Aloha shirt was sold around 1900. Some aloha shirts can cost hundreds of dollars!

Design your own aloha shirt above.

Aloha Shirt Mixup Words

How many words can you make from the letters in "aloha shirt"? Write them on the lines:

_____

_____

_____

👀 FIND IT!

Aloha shirts come in a large variety of colors and designs. Find aloha shirts with these items on them and take pictures trying on your favorites:

- ☐ Turtles
- ☐ Hula Girl
- ☐ Guitars
- ☐ Surfers
- ☐ Hawaiian Islands

SNORKELING

Tape a picture of you snorkeling.

Tip: Use an underwater camera or take a picture while on the beach wearing all your gear!

Fishy Friends

The Pacific Ocean is home to many different types of aquatic life. Write down your three favorite animals you saw while snorkeling.

_____

_____

_____

👀 FIND IT!

Look for these while you snorkel.

Hint: Snorkel Bob's shops are located all over and they give away free fish ID cards! Put one in the Souvenir Saver.

- ☐ Eel
- ☐ Sea Turtle
- ☐ Octopus
- ☐ Butterfly Fish
- ☐ Needlefish
- ☐ Angel Fish
- ☐ Jellyfish
- ☐ Shark
- ☐ Parrotfish
- ☐ Anenome
- ☐ Yellow Trumpfish
- ☐ Humuhumunukunuku

✏ WRITE IT! Silly Fish Story

Jake is a _____ and is more than ___ years old! One day, while _____ near his _____, he met a new
    type of fish   number   verb   noun

_____ named _____. Most people don't know this, but Herman is quite _____ even
type of animal   name 1   adjective

though he weighs more than 450 pounds. His new friend weighs _____ pounds and she loves to _____. At that
                                                            verb

moment a _____ named _____ jumped into the pond and yelled, "_____". Herman and
      noun   name 2   ocean   exclamation

_____ were startled and both _____. As they did, they heard laughter and realized that this was just a
name 1   verb

_____ joke. They looked at each other and _____ and then the decided to _____ happily ever after.
adjective   verb   verb

Snorkel Bob's

ABC STORE

✋ DO IT!
ABC Souvenir Design

ABC Stores are located all over Hawaii and are full of souvenirs. After searching through the stores to find the items below, create your very own souvenir that you think people would want to buy from an ABC Store in Hawaii. Decide how much you will charge for your Hawaiian souvenir.

Tape a picture of you at an ABC Store.

OPEN

ABC STORE

Tip: You can take a picture in front of the store or holding an interesting souvenir.

🔍 FIND IT!
In the ABC Store

Find these items while shopping in the ABC Stores. Take pictures of your favorite souvenirs to save in the Souvenir Saver or to tape in the pages at the back of the book.

- ☐ Macadamia nuts
- ☐ Map of Hawaii
- ☐ Key chain with your
- ☐ SPAM
- ☐ Kid crying
- ☐ Calendar with
- ☐ Starfish
- ☐ Caramacs chocolates
- ☐ Coasters with a map of the Hawaiian islands
- ☐ Dolphin pen
- ☐ Ring with flowers
- ☐ Playing cards with people in swim suits
- ☐ Bikini drinking glass
- ☐ Aloha shirt
- ☐ Shark tooth necklace

✋ DO IT! Window Shop

Browse several art galleries. Keep a list of everything you would buy, how much it cost, and put the list in the Souvenir Saver.

🖊 WRITE IT! Shopping Story

On _____, the stores are _____. I searched high and low and
   Hawaiian island   adjective

when I finally spotted a _____, I bought it! It was very _____,
        piece of art   adjective

It cost _____ dollars! I think it will look _____ and _____
     number   adjective   adjective

in my room. I cannot wait to show _____ and _____.
                     friend's name   friend's name

I know they'll look at it and _____. Next time, I'll buy a _____.
                      verb   piece of art

💲 How Expensive?

Write down the most expensive price you can find for each item as you visit art galleries:

Painting $ _____
Statue $ _____
Photograph $ _____
Cartoon Drawing $ _____
Furniture $ _____

Tape a picture of an art gallery.

Tip: Take pictures from outside the gallery and try to find an interesting sign!

WYLAND GALLERIES

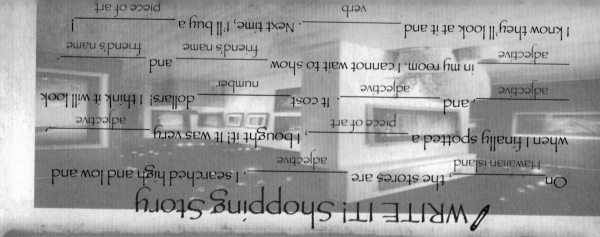

Hawaiian cuisine

? ANSWER IT! ?

Hawaiian cuisine is an interesting combination of many different types of cuisines, including American, Japanese, South Pacific and others. Many foods are similar to those you probably eat every day and some are likely very different. Answer the following questions about things you notice about Hawaiian cuisine.

List 5 menu items that you have never seen before:

_____

_____

_____

_____

The grossest menu item I found was:
_____

The most interesting menu item was:
_____

The item I wanted to try most was:
_____

Something new I tried was:
_____

Tape a picture of the most bizarre Hawaiian cuisine or menu you can find.

Tip: Sometimes our most familiar restaurants – like McDonald's or other chains – make it easiest to spot the biggest differences!

✋ DO IT!
Menu Creation

Make your own menu using the grossest, most interesting and tasty foods you found while traveling in Hawaii. Use the space on the left to create your menu.

Museum

☆ GET IT!

Put these items in the Souvenir Saver:

- ☐ Postcard
- ☐ Museum guide/map
- ☐ Museum brochure

Tape Your Entrance Ticket

Tip: If you do not have a ticket, collect a brochure.

Thu 8/14/08

The Museum of Modern

✎ WRITE IT!

Write a story about your favorite exhibit. Keep the story in the Souvenir Saver.

✋ DO IT! Artwork

Use the blank space below to draw your own masterpiece!

Tape a picture of a museum that you visited

Tip: Most museums install interesting art or landscaping near their entrances.

HONOLULU ACADEMY OF ARTS

Luau

✋ DO IT! Dancers

Luaus feature many different kinds of dancers. While watching the performers, count the number of hula dancers and the number of fire dancers. Write down the total for each and circle your favorite.

Hula Dancers
Total: _____

Fire Dancers
Total: _____

Tape a picture of the luau

Tip: You can take a picture with the dancers or even of the pig!

✏️ WRITE IT!

Imagine you are an explorer. You have sailed your ship to the middle of the Pacific Ocean and stumbled across dozens of Hawaiians hosting a luau. What would happen? Write a story about your first experience of a luau, the crazy things you saw (and did!) the food and what happened after the celebration ended. Keep your story in the Souvenir Saver.

✋ DO IT! at the Luau

Luaus are filled with interesting customs, people and food! Take a picture of each of the following and try to get yourself in as many of the pictures as possible.

☐ Hula dancer
☐ You wearing a lei
☐ Your holding a tropical drink

☐ You doing the hula
☐ Fire dancer
☐ You eating poi

☐ You with a Tiki statue
☐ Pig being cooked
☐ You with the sunset

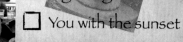

Tape a picture of the front of the aquarium or your favorite exhibit.

WAIKIKI AQUARIUM
UNIVERSITY OF HAWAII

Tip: There are many "hands-on" exhibits that make excellent photo opportunities.

✋ DO IT! Biologist

Before there were cameras, marine biologists who found strange sea creatures drew pictures and wrote descriptions to record their discoveries. Draw a picture below of a strange sea creature you find at the center. Put a written description of the animal in the Souvenir Saver.

Sea Star Challenge

Read the paragraph and and identify the parts of the Sea Star. Then color it in!
Sea Stars come in many colors, sizes and textures. Most Sea Stars, often known as Starfish, have five rays or arms that make the shape of a star. Sea Stars can have up to 50 or more rays. Each of their rays has little tubed feet along the middle and at the very end of the ray is an eye spot. In the middle of the Sea Star is it's mouth.

🔭 FIND IT!

Find and take a picture of these things!

- ☐ Sea star
- ☐ Shark
- ☐ Jellyfish
- ☐ Seahorse
- ☐ Seaweed
- ☐ Anemone
- ☐ Barnacle
- ☐ Seagull

☆ GET IT!

Collect these items during your visit!

- ☑ Brochure
- ☐ Receipt
- ☐ Postcard
- ☐ Ticket

HONOLULU ZOO

Wild Animal CHALLENGE!

Wild Animals A to Z! The Honolulu Zoo is home to animals of all different sizes, shapes, colors and...names! List animals at the zoo - one for each letter of the alphabet.

A_____ N_____
B_____ O_____
C_____ P_____
D_____ Q_____
E_____ R_____
F_____ S_____
G_____ T_____
H_____ U_____
I_____ V_____
J_____ W_____
K_____ X_____
L_____ Y_____
M_____ Z_____

Tape a picture of your favorite animal.

Tip: The animals often rest during the middle of the day. This makes it easy to take their picture!

Tape your entrance ticket or other memento.

ZOO
Admit One

DIAMOND HEAD

☆ DO IT!

There are many things to see at Diamond Head State Monument. Take pictures of the following during your visit.

- ☐ Your group before the hike
- ☐ Your group after the hike
- ☐ Warning sign
- ☐ You at the summit
- ☐ Inside the tunnel
- ☐ Waikiki Beach
- ☐ A lighthouse
- ☐ The crater

? ANSWER IT! ?

Answer the trivia questions below.

How many stairs did you climb on your journey to the top?

What is the elevation at the summit of the crater?

☆ GET IT!

Put these items from Diamond Head State Monument in the Souvenir Saver:

- ☐ Brochure
- ☐ Leaf

Tape Your Entrance Ticket

Tape a picture of Diamond Head.

Tip: You can take a picture in front of the sign, at the top or from Waikiki Beach.

DIAMOND HEAD STATE MONUMENT

PEARL HARBOR

🔍 FIND IT!
at Pearl Harbor

Pearl Harbor is a very special place. It is important that we remember all that happened here. Find the following items while visiting.

- ☐ Giant map of the Pacific Ocean
- ☐ Anchor from USS Arizona
- ☐ Photo of Battleship Row
- ☐ Submarine
- ☐ Navy plane
- ☐ Names of those who lost their lives aboard USS Arizona

Tape a picture of Pearl Harbor.

WORLD WAR II VALOR IN THE PACIFIC NATIONAL MONUMENT

Tip: The USS Arizona memorial makes a memorable place for a photo.

☆ GET IT!

At the Visitor Center, inquire about the Junior Ranger Badge. Once you earn yours, tape it here or put it in the Souvenir Saver!

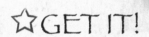

12:00

FREE TOUR TICKET

National Park Service
U.S. Department of the Interior

WWII Valor in the Pacific National Monument
Pearl Harbor, Hawai'i

- Please line up at the theater five minutes prior to your program's starting time listed above.
- Your 75 minute program consists of a film and a boat trip to the Memorial.
- No smoking, food or drinks (except water) in theater, on boat or at the Memorial.
- Audio Tour available.

♿ Accessible

Tape Your Tour Ticket

USS *Arizona* Memorial

special oHana meal

Tape a picture from the restaurant.

Tip: Some people like to take a picture of their menu, too!

🔭 FIND IT!
Special Diets

Hawaiians follow lots of diets. Find one menu item for each of the following diets:

☐ Vegan/Vegetarian

☐ Gluten-Free

☐ Lactose-Free

☐ Low Carb

☐ Organic

? ANSWER IT! ?

Our server's name was: _____

The meal I ate was: _____

It tasted: _____

It cost: _____

☆ GET IT!

Collect your receipt, a kid's menu, a coaster, and a napkin. Put them in the Souvenir Saver.

special oʜana meal

DO IT! Food Art

Draw a picture of a crazy pizza you would order and then decorate it!

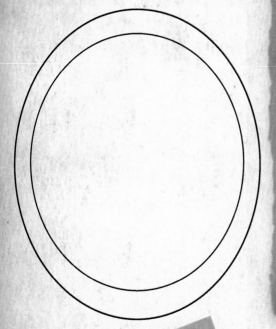

☆GET IT!

Collect your receipt, a menu, a business card, and a napkin. Put them in the Souvenir Saver or tape one here.

Tape a picture from the restaurant.

Tip: If your server is a lot of fun, try getting a picture with them!.

?? ANSWER IT! ??

Our server's name was: _____

The meal I ate was: _____

It tasted: _____

It cost: _____

ALOHA MEMORIES

Use these blank pages to tape pictures,
maps, receipts, tickets, postcards, and
anything else to remember your vacation!

POST CARD

CORRESPONDENCE   ADDRESS

THE OWL STUDIOS
JACK WEEKS & CO.
PITTSBURGH, PA.
7 Federal St.
No. 2
No. 1
105½
Smithfield St.

ALOHA MEMORIES

CORRESPONDENCE

ADDRESS